Martial Arts For Kids

Kids Activities For Healthy Kids

By
Aaron J. Perry

© 2011 by Aaron J. Perry

ISBN-13: 978-1468026795

ISBN-10: 1468026798

All Rights Reserved. No part of this publication may be reproduced in any form or by any means, including scanning, photocopying, or otherwise without prior written permission of the copyright holder.

First Printing, 2011

Printed in the United States of America

Liability Disclaimer

By reading this book, you assume all risks associated with using the advice given below, with a full understanding that you, solely, are responsible for anything that may occur as a result of putting this information into action in any way, and regardless of your interpretation of the advice.

You further agree that our company cannot be held responsible in any way for your success or failure as a result of the information presented in this book. It is your responsibility to conduct your own due diligence regarding the safety of your training and exercise if you intend to apply any of our information in any way

Before starting any new exercise you should consult your physician. If you experience any pain while following this program, do not continue. The creators, producers, participants, advertisers and distributors of this program disclaim any liabilities or loss in connection with the exercises or advice herein.

Terms of Use

You are given a non-transferable, "personal use" license to this book. You cannot distribute it or share it with other individuals.

Also, there are no resale rights or private label rights granted when purchasing this book. In other words, it's for your own personal use only.

"Discover How To Boost Your Child's Development And Give Them All The Advantages Of Becoming An Ultimate Kid That Other Parents Are Jealous Of..."

BODY * MIND * SPIRIT

Weekly Online Challenges For Kids

GO HERE NOW
↓ ↓ ↓

www.ultimatekidclub.com

About The Author

Aaron J. Perry (AJ) is a native of Auckland, New Zealand but currently lives in Brisbane, Australia.

AJ started his Martial Arts journey in 1990 and has trained in Zen Do Kai, Muay Thai and American Kenpo.

AJ began his publishing career as the author of **"Martial Games for Kids"**, an Instructors manual for making Martial Arts Lessons more enjoyable and productive for students and teachers. Visit **www.martialgames4kids.com** for more details.

AJ's other interests:

- Chairman of Martial Art Marketing, an online marketing consultant for Martial Arts School Owners.

- Owner of an MMA Clothing company that helps sponsor young MMA fighters in Australia.

- Regular official judge at Australian MMA Events (he claims it's the best seat in the house)

AJ's Official Website: **www.aaronjperry.com**

Table of Contents

Why Solo Challenges? 9
The Front Plank 11
Side Planks 13
Rocking Planks 15
Crazy Planks 17
Head Stands 19
Frozen Geckos 21
Back Bridges 23
100x Punches 25
100x Kicks 27
100x Slips 29
100x Slips 29
100x Push Ups 31
100x Squat Walk 33
Crazy Push Ups: Wide/Narrows 35
Crazy Push Ups: High/Lows 39
Crazy Push Ups: Robot Push Ups 41
Crazy Push Ups: Superman Push Ups 45
Crazy Push Ups: Hindu Push Ups 47
Crazy Push Ups: Sway Push Ups 51
Animal Moves: Duck Walks 53
Animal Moves: Bear Crawls 55
Animal Moves: Monkey Hangs 57
Animal Moves: Snake Crawls 59
Animal Moves: Worm Walking 61
Animal Moves: Spiderkid Crawls 65
Animal Moves: Kangaroo Hops 67

Why Solo Challenges?

These solo challenges have been created to develop strength, balance, co-ordination and flexibility in young martial arts students

They have also been designed to be taught by a responsible adult and then set as a challenge to be completed under adult supervision.

My goal is to help you get your kids in great shape in the fastest time possible and this means getting them to train at home which is not always an easy ask.

The "Martial Games For Kids: Kids Activities For Healthy Kids" push the competitive buttons of young kids. They are always looking to learn something new, to reach a new goal or to beat their personal best and that is what these solo challenges are all about.

All of the challenges in this book are Body-Weight exercises which is the safest form of strength training for young children. It also means you don't have to go out and buy expensive training equipment

Resistance training involving weights should be avoided during the developmental stages of youth as it applies an un-natural pressure on joints, bones, tendons and ligaments for growing bodies.

These Body-Weight exercises are also designed to be of high reps with explosive movements that can be used often because a child's body is already conditioned to their personal bodyweight.

Always use discretion on setting goals for your children and encourage them to reach new personal bests, don't compare your child with others, always acknowledge personal achievements and motivate them to achieve more.

Important Bonus:

Visit the website www.ultimatekidclub.com and give me your name and email address and in return I promise to send you a full colour eBook with more Challenges to boost your Martial Arts Training.

The Front Plank

Number of Kids: One or more
Martial Skills: Torso Strength Builder
Equipment: None

Instructions:
Lie flat on the ground, face down. Now come up onto your elbows and toes and lift your butt off the ground until your body is as straight as a plank of timber. Hold this position for 1 minute without raising your butt or dropping it to the floor.

Modifications:
It sounds easy but your body gets tired over the minute. If you struggle at first, hold the position for 20-30 seconds at a time and then keep trying to beat that time by 5 seconds until you can do a full minute.

If a minute becomes easy try doing 2 minutes straight without dropping.

Benefits:
This is a great simple challenge that will build strength in your lower back and abdominal muscles, hip flexors, legs and even your shoulders. The stronger you get the less you will shake when doing these.

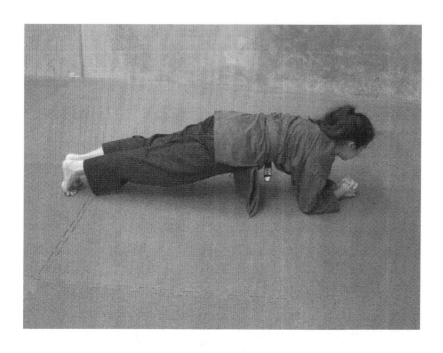

The Front Plank

Side Planks

Number of Kids: One or more
Martial Skills: Torso Strength Builder
Equipment: None

Instructions:
Lie flat on the ground, face down. Now come up onto your elbows and toes and lift your butt off the ground until your body is as straight as a plank of timber. Now turn your body sideways so that only one arm and the side of one foot is touching the ground. Keep your whole body straight, don't bow or bend up, down forward or back. Imagine a straight rod runs from your head down to your feet. Now Hold this position for 1 minute

Modifications:
The Side Plank is harder than the normal plank. If you struggle at first, hold the position for 20-30 seconds at a time and then keep trying to beat that time by 5 seconds until you can do a full minute.
If a minute becomes easy try doing 2 minutes straight without dropping.

Benefits:
This is a great simple challenge that will build strength in your lower back and abdominal muscles, obliques, hip flexors, legs and even your shoulders. The stronger you get the less you will shake when doing these.

Your oblique muscles are on the side of your body from your ribs to your hips, having strong obliques will prevent you from getting winded from hook punches and round house kicks to the ribs so I find this to be a great challenge to make you tougher during sparring and less likely to get injured from these types of strikes.

Rocking Planks

Number of Kids: One or more
Martial Skills: Torso Strength Builder
Equipment: None

Instructions:
Lie flat on the ground, face down. Now come up onto your elbows and toes and lift your butt off the ground until your body is as straight as a plank of timber for 20 seconds. Now turn your body sideways so that only one arm and the side of one foot is touching the ground. Keep your whole body straight, don't bow or bend up, down, forward or back and hold this position for 20 seconds then rock to your other side and hold that side plank for 20 seconds.

Modifications:
Because you've already been doing the single challenges this should be an easy one so to make this more challenging see how many of these you can do before you lose control and touch the ground or shake too much.

This is a great mini challenge to do during the Ad breaks when you watch your favourite TV show, see if you can do it for the whole Ad break.

Benefits:
This challenge will build strength in your lower back and abdominal muscles, obliques, hip flexors, legs and even your shoulders. It will also get

your body used to moving from one position to another with good balance and control. The stronger you get the less you will shake when doing these.

As you strengthen your abdominals and obliques you will be able to handle punches and kicks during sparring without injury. If your classmates don't do these then you will have a big advantage during sparring sessions.

Go From Side To Front To Other Side And Back Again.

Crazy Planks

Number of Kids: One or more
Martial Skills: Torso Strength Builder
Equipment: None

Instructions:
These are called crazy Planks because you have to be crazy to do them
Lie flat on the ground, face down. Now come up onto your elbows and toes and lift your butt off the ground until your body is as straight as a plank of timber for 30 seconds. Now turn your body sideways so that only one arm and the side of one foot is touching the ground. Keep your whole body straight, don't bow or bend up, down, forward or back and hold this position for 30 seconds. Now keep rotating in the same direction so that you are looking up to the sky, have both feet flat on the floor and your elbows or hands, keep your butt raised off the ground so your upper legs, stomach and chest are flat like a table top and hold this for 30 seconds.
Now rock to your other side and hold that side plank for 30 seconds and then return to the normal plank starting position for another 30 seconds.

Modifications:
This is like the Rocking Planks but much harder on your muscles because of the table plank and it should take you 2 minutes to do one of these. By now you should be getting really strong so see

how many of these you can do before you lose control and touch the ground or shake too much.

Benefits:
This challenge will build strength in your lower back and abdominal muscles, hip flexors, obliques, lower back, legs and even your shoulders. This will greatly improve core strength and keep you much safer during your martial arts training and sparring.

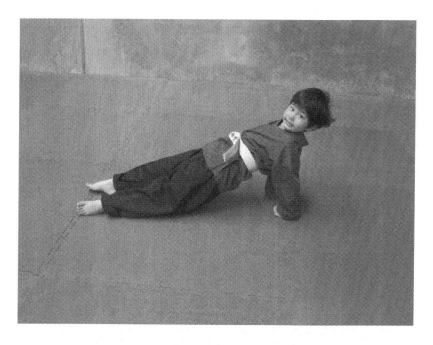

Reverse Plank (AKA Table Top or Slide)

Head Stands

Number of Kids: One or more
Martial Skills: Neck, shoulder strength and balance
Equipment: Matts, grass area or small pillow

Instructions:
Kneel down on the ground and touch your forehead on the ground. Place your hands on the ground in line with your chin similar to doing a push-up. Now keep your feet on the ground but move your knees to rest them on the back of your elbows. From here you should be able to lift your feet of the ground and have all the weight on your head and hands.
When you feel balanced try moving your legs off your elbows and up into the air... You're now doing a head stand.
Try and hold a balanced position for a full minute.

Modifications:
If you find it easy to get into a headstand and stay balanced then try moving your legs around. Spread them sideways and front and back.
If you have a friend with you, get them to put a basketball or soccer ball on top of your feet when you are in position and try not to let the ball drop before your 1 minute is up.

Benefits:
Neck Strength is very important for all fighting arts. If your not sure if your neck is strong enough when you first start trying this challenge get a friend to hold your legs and take some of your weight and help balance you.
Having a strong neck will save you from injuries during training.

Head Stand With Hands Placed Forward for Correct BalanceAnd Control.

Frozen Geckos

Number of Kids: One or more
Martial Skills: Core strength
Equipment: None

Instructions:
A Gecko is a small lizard that runs really quickly on all four legs but if you startle them they will freeze on the spot and stay motionless hoping that you don't notice them.

For this challenge get into a push up position, when you think your balanced lift your right hand and your left foot off the ground and bend your leg, then don't move, stay still just like a gecko for 30 seconds.
Go back to your push-up position and now raise your left hand and your right foot off the ground and hold it for 30 seconds.

Modifications:
As you get stronger and your balance improves try and hold each position for a full minute. Then to make it even harder, swap quickly from one position to the other ten times before freezing. This will really test your strength and balance.

Benefits:
Cross balancing like this uses all your core muscles at the same time and really helps strengthen the small support muscles running along your spine which will give you great power when grap-

pling or throwing punches and kicks.

Back Bridges

Number of Kids: One or more
Martial Skills: Core strength, Flexability
Equipment: None

Instructions:
To do a back bridge you want to lie down on your back and try to put your hands palm down flat on the ground close to your head. Now bring your feet up close to your butt on your tip toes. When your ready curve your back and raise your belly up toward the sky as high as you can get it so only your feet, hands and the top of your head is touching the ground.
Try and hold this for a full minute.

Modifications:
If you struggle to hold it for a whole minute start with 20-30 seconds and then build up. When you can easily do a minute try doing 2-3 minutes.

*Advanced option: You can try holding this position without any hands but only try this when you have a strong neck and you have warmed up properly.

Make sure there is an adult watching you to make sure you are doing this safely.

Benefits:
Back bridges improve flexibility in the back and neck. They also stretch the abdominal muscles and open the chest up for deeper breathing which is great for overall health. Bridging is also a great technique used in ground fighting to get leverage for rolling or escaping from your opponent.

Back Bridges

100x Punches

Number of Kids: One or more
Martial Skills: Punching Techniques
Equipment: None

Instructions:
To join the 100 Club means you need to be able to do a technique properly 100x. This is a solo challenge but it is good if you have someone that can keep count or hold a focus pad or shield for you to strike.
If you are by yourself, throw the punches in the air but don't extend your arm all the way out till it's straight or beyond because you may hurt your arm.

The idea of this challenge is for you to do 100 perfect punches. What I mean by perfect punches is that you start in your ready position and then throw your punch, immediately returning to your ready position.
If you have a partner ask them to check that you always return to your ready position before throwing your next punch.
It is really important that you do a perfect punch each time for 100 times... Doing 100 sloppy punches is a complete waste of time, so focus when you do this.

Modifications:
The 100x Punch challenge can be done with a variety of punches: jabs, hooks, upper-cuts, straight punch, back-fist, palm strikes, overhead claws, knife hand, hammer fist...

*Advanced option: If you're good at single punches try the same challenge with combinations. Here are some options:

Jab, straight
Jab, straight, upper-cut
Low jab, upper-cut, hook
Jab, straight, hook, upper-cut
Jab, Straight, low hook

Benefits:
Practicing your punches 100x properly will train your muscle memory so that having good form, proper body movement becomes something you don't have to think about.
Remember to train with good technique otherwise if you train 100x sloppy punches then you will always do sloppy punches.

100x Kicks

Number of Kids: One or more
Martial Skills: Kicking Technique
Equipment: None

Instructions:
This is a solo challenge but it is good if you have someone that can keep count or hold a focus pad or boxing bag for you.
The idea of this challenge is for you to do 100 perfect kicks. What I mean by perfect kick is that you start in your ready position and then throw your kick just how your instructor taught you and then immediately return to your ready position.
If you have a partner ask them to check that you are doing the kick correctly and the you always return to your ready position before throwing your next kick.
It is really important that you do a perfect kick each time for 100 times... Doing 100 sloppy kicks is also a complete waste of time, so focus when you do this.

Modifications:
The 100x kick challenge is harder than the punches because it takes more energy to throw your legs. It ay seem easy for the first 20 but the last 20 will be hard. Make sure you don't lose focus and get sloppy.

The 100x can be done with a variety of kicks: straight kick, round house, side kick, spinning heel kick, crescent kick, sweeps, chicken kicks, axe kicks...

*Advanced option: If you're good at single kicks try the same challenge with combinations. Here are some options:

Front straight kick, rear leg roundhouse
Rear side kick, land then rear front kick
Rear roundhouse to spinning hook kick
Front kick to rear leg chicken kick

Benefits:
Practicing your kicks 100x properly will train your muscle memory so that having good form, proper body movement becomes something you don't have to think about. Now your hands and your feet should both be great weapons.

Remember to train with good technique otherwise if you train 100x sloppy kicks then you will always do sloppy kicks.

Note: "Don't fear the person that has trained 10,000 kicks... Fear the person that has trained one kick 10,000 times."

100x Slips

Number of Kids: One or more
Martial Skills: Slipping and Punching Techniques
Equipment: String or thin rope

Instructions:
This is a cool boxing challenge for you.
Tie a piece of string between two objects at your shoulder height when you are in your fighting guard. You can use posts or trees, whatever you can find to tie the string to at the right height but try to give your self plenty of room to move under the string on both sides.
Now stand in your fighting guard wit the string on your right shoulder next to your ear. Now bob down under the string, just enough to clear it, move to your right and pop back up in your fighting guard so the string is on your left shoulder just by your ear. Now bob back down and slip back to your original position and that is one slip. Do this 100x, keep your balance and move your feet slightly if you have to.

** Always keep your eyes facing forward to where the string is tied. If you look down at the ground when you are slipping you may get punched by an opponent without ever seeing it coming. Use your legs and back to duck under the string but always keep your head facing forwards.**

Modifications:
Slipping is a Boxing technique for avoiding punches. Practice moving your head just low enough to avoid touching the string, don't do huge movements as this will burn your energy and probably put you off balance.

When you are good at slipping, start adding in some punches while your head is on each side of he string.

Throw a jab, slip to the right and throw a jab then a straight and then slip back to your left and immediately throw an upper-cut.

Benefits:
This is a great drill to prepare for sparring. It gets you used to moving your head which makes it a harder target to hit for your opponent. When you learn to slip and punch at the same time you will be able to counter punch your opponent more easily.

100x Push Ups

Number of Kids: One or more
Martial Skills: Upper body strength and punching power
Equipment: none

Instructions:
100x Push Ups is not an easy challenge
To start with I want you to do 100 push-ups during a single day, so that may be 15-20 every hour until you've done 100.
It may be 30 in the morning, 40 at lunch and 30 more before dinner. Break it up however you need to get 100 done in a day.
As you get stronger make it 50 then anther 50 after a 10-15 minute rest.
Then maybe 70 followed buy 30 more after a 5 minute rest
Before you know it you will be able to do 100 push ups in a single go.

"Make sure that you always do proper push ups, all the way down and all the way up. If you cheat by doing half push ups, or just bobbing your head or any other way of cheating then you won't benefit from this challenge."

I need you to complete this challenge because I can't let you do the 100x Sprawl challenge until I know you can easily do the 100x Push up challenge.

Modifications:
Normal push ups are good to start with but there are a huge variety of push ups available that will really test your strength and focus.

High/Low push ups
Wide/Narrow push ups
Slip push ups
Robot Push ups
Clappers
High Five push ups
Hindu push ups...

Benefits:
Push ups develop upper body strength which boosts punching power when done properly. They also help with opening the chest for deeper breathing and some of the variations listed above will improve flexibility and explosive power.

100x Squat Walk

Number of Kids: One or more
Martial Skills: Leg strength, balance
Equipment: open area

Instructions:
This challenge sounds easy but it isn't.
Find some space where you can walk in a straight line on flat ground.
Start with your feet together and then take a big step forward with one leg and as your foot touches the ground lower your body down until the knee of your back leg just touches the ground. Make sure you keep your back straight and your head up looking straight ahead while you do it. Now use your leg muscles to push your body back up and take a big step forward with your other leg and then lower your body till the other knee just lightly touches the ground.

Do this for 100x steps without falling over.

Modifications:
With a bit of practice this challenge will become easy for you so there are two ways to make this challenge even harder.

1. Do the squat walks in an area that goes up-hill. Start with a slight up-hill area and then try a steeper area when it becomes easier.

2. Do one leg for the first 50 then the other leg for the second 50. This means after each step you come back up and bring your back foot up to your front foot and then step forward with the same foot again and again for 50-100 steps before changing to the other leg stepping forward.

Benefits:
This will really test your leg strength and your balance. It sounds easy but when your legs start getting tired you will probably lose your balance and fall over.
The power you use to lift your body up with your legs will help you throw stronger front kicks and do more explosive takedowns if you do these in your martial art training.

Crazy Push Ups: Wide/Narrows

Number of Kids: One or more
Martial Skills: Upper body Strength
Equipment: Grass or matted area

By now you should be really strong and find normal push-ups too easy to do so now I'll start showing you some Crazy Push-Ups to really test you.

Instructions:
Get into your normal push-up starting position. Now spread your hands out wider by about two hand spaces on each side, this is the position of your hands for a wide push-up. Lower yourself down and then push yourself up as fast as you can so that your body pops up in the air and you can bring your hands in close together so that your thumbs are nearly touching and then lower yourself back down.

When your hands are close together directly under your chest tis is the position for your narrow push-up.

Push yourself back up again as fast as you can so that you can move your hands back out to the

wide position while your body has popped up into the air.
Try and do these quickly and make them flow from the wide to the narrow to the wide to the narrow... For 10 times.
(Doing a wide and a narrow push-up counts as one)

Modifications:
These push-ups are hard enough for now so keep them simple and see how many you can do before your arms are too tired to push you up quickly enough to more your hands to the next position.

Benefits:
The wide/narrow push-up works different areas of the upper body.
The wide works on the chest (pectoral muscles) and shoulders (front deltoid muscles) while the narrow push-ups build strength in your arms (triceps muscles)
The quick explosive power you need to do these push-ups is the same needed for strong punches and pushes. The wide push-ups also builds strength that you will use when grappling with someone, trying to push and pull them from side to side to get them off balance for a takedown or throw.

Wide Push Up Hand Position

Narrow Push Up Hand Position

Crazy Push Ups: High/Lows

Number of Kids: One or more
Martial Skills: Upper body Strength
Equipment: Grass or matted area

Instructions:
Get into your normal push-up starting position. Now move one hand forward so that it is inline with the top of your head and move your other hand backward so that it is inline with your ribs. This is your new starting position.
Lower yourself down then push yourself back up quickly so that you can slide your hands the opposite position. The high hand moves down to your ribs and the low hand moves up in line with your head.
Lower yourself back down and the push up quickly and move your hands back to the original high/low positions.

Try and do these quickly and make them flow from one high/low to the next... For 10 times. (A high/low push-up has two push-ups to count as one set.))

Modifications:
These push-ups are hard enough for now so keep them simple and see how many you can do before your arms are too tired to push you up quickly enough to more your hands to the next position.

Benefits:
The High/Low push-up works different areas of the upper body.
The unbalanced position of the hands causes your back and core muscles to work harder to keep you balanced. They also strain the upper and lower areas of the chest muscles (pectorals) which will improve the strength of your hammering blocks and your uppercut punches.

One Hand High And One Hand Low

Crazy Push Ups: Robot Push Ups

Number of Kids: One or more
Martial Skills: Upper Body and Core Strength
Equipment: Grass or matted area

Instructions:
Get into your normal push-up starting position. Now this is how you do a Robot Push-up... Lift your right hand off the ground and drop down onto your right elbow, now lift your left hand off the ground and drop onto your left elbow... Now push yourself back up on your right hand side to get your right hand back in the normal position and the push up to get your left hand back in the normal position... That was a Robot push up.

It's a simple exercise but a great one for Martial Artists.

Try and do 50 in one go. Do 25 in each direction.

Modifications:
These push-ups are awesome for working your arms, chest and obliques. If you find 50 too easy then try 100 without stopping.

Benefits:
The movement of this push-up requires you to twist your body as you do them and this means you are strengthening your side stomach muscles (your obliques). This challenge will help you put more power into your hooks and wrestling/grappling/judo throws.

Start In Normal Push Up Position...

Crazy Push Ups: Superman Push Ups

Number of Kids: One or more
Martial Skills: Upper Body and Core Strength
Equipment: Grass or matted area

Instructions:
Get into your normal push-up starting position. At the top of the push-up position raise your right hand and your left leg (bend it at the knee) and do a Superman pose as if you are flying for 5 seconds, then do a normal push-up and at the top lift your left hand and right leg as if you are flying and hold it for 5 seconds.
Doing both sides counts as 1 Superman push-up. Try and do 50 and if you find that easy then try 100.

Modifications:
If you want to make these harder then keep the superman pose as you lower yourself down into the lower push-up position and only put both hands and feet on the ground at the bottom of the push-up

Benefits:
Superman push-ups require balance and core body strength to hold the flying position and it may not seem that hard to do but it uses a lot of small muscles running up your spine which are very important for strengthening your core and protecting your back from damage during your martial art training.

Push Up And Fly Like Superman!

Crazy Push Ups: Hindu Push Ups

Number of Kids: One or more
Martial Skills: Upper Body and Deep Breathing
Equipment: Grass or matted area

Instructions:
These are some killer push-ups and they work all your muscles and stretch your body at the same time.

Start in a normal push-up position and then raise your butt up to the ceiling and straighten your arms so your body forms an upside down V shape.
Now bend your arms so your head comes close down to the ground, keep lowering your butt as your nose slides forward just above the ground... Get your butt as low as it goes without touching the ground and then look up and straighten your arms and bend your back so you can look straight up in the sky.
Hold it for a second then keep your arms straight and raise your butt back as high as possible to return to your starting position.

Hindu Push-ups should be done quickly. Breath in as you form the upside down V and then breathe out as you scoop forward and look up to the sky.

Modifications:
As you do this push-up you will increase your flexibility so as you get better at them, start moving your hands and feet closer together so you can get more stretch as you do these push-ups

Benefits:
Hindu Push-Ups are commonly used by Indian Wrestlers. They are great for strengthening a lot of muscle groups and at the same time they improve flexibility and the deep breathing exercise is great for circulation and general health.

Hindu Push Up Starting Position...

Middle of Hindu Push Up

End Position Of Hindu Push Up, Look Up To The Sky

Crazy Push Ups: Sway Push Ups

Number of Kids: One or more
Martial Skills: Upper Body Strength
Equipment: Grass or matted area

Instructions:
I think these are the toughest push-ups of all time which is why I'm giving them to you last.

Start in your normal push-up position. Now from the top position, move your body to the right so your right hand is in the narrow push up position and your left hand is in the wide push-up position. Now lower your right side down first then your left (similar to a robot push-up). Now as your body is flat to the floor, move your body across to the left while keeping it as close to the ground as possible so that you left hand is now in the narrow position and your right hand is in the wide position. Now push yourself up to the normal top position.
From there do the same thing in reverse, dropping down on your left, shifting across to your right and coming back up to the top position.
That is a Sway Push-up and they are HARD!!!
Do them slowly, don't rush through them as you will be cheating.

Modifications:
No modifications for these, just see how many you can do before you collapse.

Benefits:
These evil push-ups use all your chest and shoulder muscles. The slower you do them the better they are for you. They work the chest, shoulders and stomach like no other push-up I've ever tried.

Sway From One Side To The Other With Each Push Up.

Animal Moves: Duck Walks

Number of Kids: One or more
Martial Skills: Leg Strength
Equipment: Matted floor/grass area

Instructions:
I'm sure you've seen a Duck walk... They waddle along on little legs with their butt shaking behind them. They have webbed feet which means they can't walk like we do because they would trip over all the time... But I can tell you how to walk like a duck.

Squat down on the balls of your feet with your butt low to the ground and your back as straight as you can (don't be all bent over looking at the ground) keep your head up and look straight ahead.

Now keep your butt low to the ground and try walking forwards. Just take small steps. Because your legs are really bent you can't walk like you normally would, you need to shift your weight over to one side so you can move your other foot. The more you move your butt and waddle the easier it is to move around quickly.

It may seem crazy when you first try it but that's

some of the fun. Keep trying and it will soon become easy.

Modifications:
When you get comfortable waking around in a flat area with the Duck Walk, try doing it in a hilly area. This challenge gets a whole lot harder when the ground is un-even.
Also try moving forwards, backwards and sideways or walk quickly along a zigzagging path.

Benefits:
Duck walking really improves leg strength and flexibility in your hips, legs and back. Doing it often will build strength and balance. Get used to doing it by yourself and then you will be better prepared for the partner and group games where you try and knock over your friends while you are all duck walking.

Animal Moves: Bear Crawls

Number of Kids: One or more
Martial Skills: All over Strength
Equipment: Matted floor/grass area

Instructions:
Big Grizzly Bears and Polar Bears are really powerful animals.

Walking like a Bear means you have to move around on all four legs (your legs and your arms) all the time... But Bears are different to dogs and horses because their legs don't bend much... So to walk/crawl like a bear you have to get down on all fours and take longer strides with your arms and legs almost straight.

Modifications:
Try walking around like this for a full minute, it's hard at first, your arms and shoulders get tired quickly.
When you need a rest either lower yourself down to the ground to pause for a few seconds or push your self up onto your back legs and raise your front paws in the air and growl like a bear before dropping back down to your normal bear walking

Benefits:
Bear crawls are great for building arm and shoulder strength and stretching your back and legs. Becoming strong and balanced in this stance will help you with your grappling when you end up on all fours.

Animal Moves: Monkey Hangs

Number of Kids: One or more
Martial Skills: Upper Body Strength, Grip strength
Equipment: Monkey bars, jungle gym, pull up bar...

Instructions:
Hanging around like a monkey is all about having fun and just hanging around.
Find somewhere that you can hang from with your arms straight and your feet won't touch the ground. If you're lucky you may have a swing set in the backyard or a jungle gym in your local park.
Monkey Hangs mean you swing around on the bar while hanging on as long as you can without touching the ground.

Modifications:
If you have a good area to do monkey hangs then try swing from one spot to another, hang from one arm for a while and when the arm is getting tired swap to your other arm. Try pulling your body up so you can look over the bar you're hanging from. Keep moving around and swap your hand positions from close together to spreading them far apart.

Benefits:
Having a really strong grip is a big bonus in your martial art. It means you will have strong punches and you can hang on to people if you do any ground fighting.

Hanging from the bars also helps strengthen your arm, chest, shoulder and back muscles which will help protect you from injuries when you are training hard and sparring.

Animal Moves: Snake Crawls

Number of Kids: One or more
Martial Skills: Upper Body Strength
Core muscles
Equipment: Grass or matted area

Instructions:
Note: Wear old clothes if you do this on the grass because they will get really dirty and I don't want you getting in trouble.

To do snake crawls you have to use your arms to drag your body around.
You have to stay low to the ground at all times, now use your forearms to drag your body forward. Reach out and put your forearm on the ground in front of you and pull yourself forward while stretching out with your other arm to get it on the ground further in front and keep using each arm, one after the other to crawl like a snake.

- You can't cheat and lift yourself over the ground raising your chest by putting your hands down, snakes don't have arm so you have to stay low.
- You can't use your legs to help move you forward because snakes don't have legs either, so just let your legs drag behind you.

Modifications:
Try making an obstacle course for yourself to get through using your snake crawling skills. Find some objects that you can place to create a path that you have to snake crawl around or under or over.

Benefits:
When you get really good at snake crawls you will be able to move very quickly along the ground just using your arms. This is a great skill to have if you ever need to chase someone after you have been knocked down.

These snake crawls builds upper body strength and the slithering movement, wiggling your body to get your arms out in front helps stretch and strengthen your back and hips.

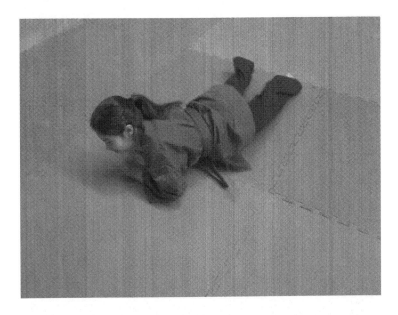

Animal Moves: Worm Walking

Number of Kids: One or more
Martial Skills: Upper Body Strength, Core muscles
Equipment: Grass or matted area

Instructions:
Note: Wear old clothes if you do this on the grass because they will get really dirty and I don't want you getting in trouble.

- The worm is different to the snake

To do the "Worm" you need to lie face down and stretch out your arms and legs in a straight line. Now join your hands together and keep your legs close together. Use your forearms on the ground to pull your whole body forward until your chest is over the top of your hands.

Now keep your arms and knees where they are on the ground but lift your butt and chest up of the ground and back towards your feet. Now quickly push your upper body higher off the ground with your arms and push forward from your knees and lower legs and stretch out your arms so that you are fully stretched when you land flat on your belly... That's ONE Worm Crawl.

Keep repeating this to crawl along your path.

Modifications:
Try making an obstacle course for yourself to get through using your snake crawling skills. Find some objects that you can place to create a path that you have to snake crawl around or over.

Benefits:
Worm crawls are a fun way to get stronger but they can also be used as a very dangerous move to knock someone off their feet. I'm not going to explain how to do that because it is very dangerous so if you want to know then ask your instructor to show you how to do it safely.

Animal Moves: Spiderkid Crawls

Number of Kids: One or more
Martial Skills: Full Body Strength, core muscles, balance
Equipment: Grass or matted area

Instructions:
Spiderkid crawls are a type of push-up crawl and they are one of the hardest to do... But by now you should be as strong as the Incredible Hulk so I'll tell you how to do them...

Lie face down and get into your Superman push-up position with one arm and one leg in the air... Now lower your body so it is just off the ground and stretch out your floating arm and bend your knee to bring your floating leg closer towards your hand on the ground. Now put your floating hand and foot on the ground and lift up your other hand and foot while keeping your body really low and then repeat the movements again and again to spider crawl across the room.

Modifications:
The slower you do this the harder it is, so try and move slowly without losing your balance. It should take at least 5 seconds to change from one position to the next.

Keep LOW and move SLOW! Pretend your sneaking up on your prey ;-)

Benefits:
I warned you that these would be hard.
They use all your new strength and balance skills to their maximum.

Animal Moves: Kangaroo Hops

Number of Kids: One or more
Martial Skills: Leg Strength, Core muscles, balance
Equipment: Grass or matted area

Instructions:
A Kangaroo is an Australian Animal that hops around on big powerful legs.

Stand with your feet shoulder width apart and facing straight ahead.
Keep your elbows tucked in tight to your ribs and bend your hands are up almost like a fighting stance. (Have you ever heard of the Boxing Kangaroos?)
Now bend your knees so that you are squatting down about halfway, lean forward and then push off with both legs at the same time to hop as far as you can.
Try doing 10-20 of these to get used to hopping. Don't swing your arms, keep them in the same position and let your legs do all the work.

Modifications:
When you think you have the hopping, the landing and your balance all sorted try hopping continuously. You should be able to get even further as you build up momentum.

When you're ready set up a course to hop around and put down some obstacles to hop over. Use cardboard boxes or a pile of folded towels. Don't use any hard solid objects with sharp corners or fragile things that will break if you accidentally land on them.

Benefits:
Kangaroos can hop huge distances 30-40 feet in a single jump if they need to and you can see how big and strong their legs are.

These kangaroo Hops will boost your leg power which means you will be able to jump higher and kick much harder when you are doing your martial art moves.

Also, because this is an explosive muscle movement it will give you explosive power to charge in on your opponent for a takedown or to move in quickly for a jab or striking combo.

If You Have A Friend Then Make It A Race.

Frequently Asked Questions

How often should my child do these Challenges?

These are all flexibility and body weight exercises so they are safe for your child to perform as often as they can handle. Different kids have different energy levels. I suggest setting a list of challenges for them and then ticking them off as they are completed each day.

Can my child combine these Challenges?

Yes, the challenges in this book utilize different muscle groups so it is a good idea to to combine several challenges to provide a well balanced training routine for your child.

Are back bridges safe for children?

Back bridges are a great exercise for children and adults. Back bridges help with flexibility, spinal alignment and blood flow. I know it looks crazy and painful from the photos in this book. The students used for these photos are very healthy so don't be disappointed if you struggle with this exercise at first. Everybody is different so do what you can and if you feel any pain stop immediately.

What age group is this for?

This book was initially designed for young students (4yo-15yo) but these Challenges are also used by a lot of adult students. Bodyweight exercises are the safest way to build strength, flexibility and speed for all age groups.

Where can I find more Challenges for my child?

You can find more Challenges for your child at **www.ultimatekidclub.com**, this website has been specially designed to help build the Body, Mind and Spirit of Children involved in Martial Arts.

Visit **www.ultimatekidclub.com** and give me your name and email address and in return I promise to send you a full colour eBook with more Challenges to boost their Martial Arts Training and help build strong character values to turn them into an "Ultimate Kid".

Acknowledgements

I would like to thank the Cameron Family for allowing me to photograph them for this book and the others in the **"Martial Arts For Kids"** series.

I would also like to thank all of the other people I have trained with over the years that have helped me become a well rounded fighter and person. I always try to improve but the more I learn the more I realize I don't know, and I now know for certain that there are always people bigger, tougher, smarter, faster and more talented than me which keeps my ego in check. It's an honour to have met and trained with you...

Don and Suzanne Woods (and their 3 kids), Jeff Speakman (so generous with your knowledge), Allan Cable, Michael Inwood, Zav, Ross Cameron (his entire family and the Fightcross MMA Fight Team)

I'd also like to thank Rick Kirkham, Richard Hackworth and John Graden for their continous support and promotion of the **Martial Games for Kids** system that has now spread around the world and is being used by 100's (possibly 1000's) of Martial Arts Instructors across a wide variety of martial arts styles to help excite kids into training harder and achieving their black belt.

Further Information

For further information about products and services from Aaron J. Perry or Martial Art Marketing please visit the following websites...

www.martialartforkids.com
For more information about this series of Martial Arts For Kids books

www.aaronjperry.com
For general information about the author of this book.

www.martialgames4kids.com
AJ's first manual for Martial Arts Instructors has been continually updated and expanded to help Martial Arts Schools grow their classes and get more kids to stick with their martial art training to black belt level and beyond.

www.martialartmarketing.com
For information about online and offline marketing for Martial Arts School Owners

Made in the USA
Lexington, KY
11 January 2014